# How to Board a Moving Ship

Rikki Santer

LILY POETRY REVIEW BOOKS

## Also by Rikki Santer:

Published by Lily Poetry Review Books
223 Winter Street
Whitman, MA 02382

https://lilypoetryreview.blog/

ISBN: 978-1-7365990-6-8

Cover design: Martha McCollough
Cover art: detail from "Barrel in the Waves", Ivan Bilibin

# Contents

# How to Board a Moving Ship

## Now Half as Much

The largesse of a rivulet is to be fully herself—a cocktail
        of muchness—flora & fauna freckling her lips &
tongue.  Summer days I scraped my knees keeping up with
        her span, collie-mix at my side in pesky confederation.
We liked rocks turned over, the flavor of the wind, my big toe
        stirring clouds afloat in rhinestone ripples.  School with
its flinty diction & guardrail lessons rusted me in groundwater,
        so local library with its deep planets was my lodestar—
more rocks to overturn, bravery for giggling in church.
        Fizzie tabs & blue raspberry Kool-Aid—magic potions
to muster power—neighborhood jerks knew the tingling
        slaps from my stained lips.  Now turn, ladies & gentlemen,
to the sieve of my nimbleness as it stalks my back door where
        a dimming flood light stays lit for slow motion & delay.

## Alteration Love Finds

Neighbors turn into bears, golden vanilla coats, curried
yawns, yellow teeth. We stroll through backyards, around
boxwood fences. At the party we hunker into a worn couch
inside a screened front porch. It's a plague, someone mutters,
wash your hands in ways you've never done before.
In the morning, I'm a banshee snoring. Bursts of tiny breaths
against our pitted cheeks, mouths dry with sand. Outside
the kitchen window, the clothesline shapes the dialectic:
panties still dependable as lust? Next to the sink, cell phone
like a dying cicada. I fill empty bread bags with dirt to freeze
for what winter will implore. At a green light the accelerator pedal
flaps impotent. Fiat sputters while bears converge, plastic wine
bottles like tumbleweed. My elbow swollen hot & tight with fool's
inversion. Soon my body no longer contains its wound. Pus waters
our front lawn cactus which expresses itself by growing thorns.

# Enough

What do jackrabbits know
their hind legs like hands
across the desert my palm
across your belly, accordion
of your sleep we dream
petroglyphs signaling red rover
across the escarpment
specks of silica sparkle
our path a rattle snake
autographs its crossing.

What does the spider know
asterisk in our bathtub.
Kitchen windows steam tonight
like mirrors that have had enough
of sour debates & cursive wounds
from our married snouts.
Domestic bonds suspend us
like marionette strings
freshly cut asters aren't enough
to evaporate shadows on
streaked walls of disagreement.

Yet beauty is always passing.
Outside two mule deer
& absolution at the creek,
their ears swivel, our eyes
moist around the rims.

## How to Board a Moving Ship

*Vertigo benign* entwines two clocks—
            my inner debates my outer
    shaker full of crystals wagering
                who will slice this cauliflower
      with serrated gone fool
              yellow my ambitions
        green my decisions
                    blue my sagging sleep.

If I look in the bathroom mirror long enough
    memory will secrete its dissonance
        seeping like greasy lightning
    my head inside a Graviton
    skirts of light tumble
            through my skull spinning like a plate.

In the living room aquarium, my marine sister upside-down for weeks—
    Oranda water puppy, oversized wen anchors her all day belly-up
        she struggles to right herself, fins Morse code distress
    black eyes meet mine through water & glass.

                    I'd like to glide again:
                    bourbon snifter affording transparency
                    sandcastle totem affording horizon.
My mother returns much younger than I
    treading a path around  & around Wade Park Lagoo
        fresh from a doctor's delivery of a life
    sentence, scars on her nerve fibers
        creeping like algae.

I doze, dream, a dervish virgin
      twirling in my childhood rooster dress, emerald green anklets,
          my compass gyrates against a craggy atlas.

Oranda nestles into my cupped hand as I hold her upright in her tank.
      Her body relaxes.
                  We board our moving ship.

## Feathers

*after Ligaya Misham*

I'm riddled with pinions.
Some mornings I feel your ghost
heartbeat, tiny bird deep
inside my body—
you parachuted
when the storm
of my mother's sudden
death made landfall.  I collect
plumes from passing vultures
their mythology ignores me
but I am tethered
to their hunger for the dead.
I never named you
but I knew your way
the fractal life for the brother
you left behind.

Half leaves, half sails
bouquets of sluffed feathers
on my nightstand
my porch
totems on my window sills
dormant quills
to right my sorrow
with the smallest of filaments
held together
by microscopic hooks.

## Much Morning

Soft tones swan up from backyard bowels,
tender pulse of a waking ravine. Through
nostrils of garden a hummingbird orbits
my socked ankles, drunk on red, in fetch
of dawn. Inside, a phone call from miles
so far away. My birthday ruptures and stains.
*Your mother's gone in wheelchair slumber,*
*head collapsed forward into her lilac pillow,*
*hands the folded birds in her lap.* My uterus
spits tremors, her first grandchild's embryo
can't weather the storm. I stumble into
the swells of morning. Hummingbird darts
to a stand of shagbark hickories steady
in sunlight, and in the shadows, a birth/
death anniversary throbs, readying for a
lifetime's return, braided tight.

## Hymn

Thirsty for a
Pleistoncene morning,
    I'm a graying creature
trotting in & out of shadows.

        I rest deep
            in the dark belly
      of my backyard ravine.
           Needy seeds float

      in the chilled mist,
my low howl stirs
    the sternum,
my ears swivel

        for footsteps—
           wild crones who live
        at the end of time, carry
           lupine bundles for healing,

     & not afraid to bite back.
Wolf birds pick
    at the bones
of my story,

        death is our living,
           to love sky & creek
      so much sometimes
        I cannot bear it.

To track & run,
summon & repel
        prepare to find
my luminous pack

            & fetch
                the feeder root
            with sponges
                of my worn paws.

## Pro Bono Messengers in Baltimore

I squeeze a lima bean between my thumb
& index finger & with just the right amount
of pressure its slimy heart sails across the room.
We're sisters, I think.  Lizard's severed tail,
small as my toenail, turquoise & rolling
over linoleum for a life of its own beyond
another Instagram dopamine drip.
Tap shoes still haunt me when I clicked
for my parents' living room guests.
Cut to today's neighbor, sleeveless t-shirt,
arms like skewers, fleshy baritone as the elevator
delivers her to the rest of her tale.  Everything
in this world can be folded.  Could that red bug
on the neighbor's porch be a blood droplet
or does it dart like a cursor to undercut
belief?  Giant roach on my ceiling, a planet
collecting story lines that I store with frayed
rubber bands.  Then the earthy liquor of midnight
beans when I can finally reach a distant beach,
which is to say my tiny back stoop, where moths
orbiting, never mistake brilliance.

## Dream Recurring

I live in a foreign house where I never reside,
     except in reruns that come around too often
          to suspend and stall me.  My everything's in
        there—furniture, cats, boyfriend whispers, but
    sometimes stuff that isn't, like this morning's
          motorcycle panting in the hallway, grimy work
gloves pinned to the wall—my curator's brio.

          At the end of a cul-de-sac, the front yard
      overgrown with shrubbery, edges blur,
    haunted like a Google street view—yet
        there I am, young girl swinging swinging
     a rusty gate, a sun fringed in fog, and
        heaps of loose keys under blooming
  redbud. On a familiar kitchen counter,
dog-eared catalogue of mail-order firecrackers,
        porcelain bowl teetering with pimento tongues.
    I cha-cha-slide on chessboard floor as a troupe
of three-legged Maine Coons weaves around me.

    What's really snagged in these brimming
       baskets of recall?  Spent tampons gnarl
        in bathroom sink, plastic shower curtain
          busy with squirrels, boyfriend fingernails—
gruff and ready—retrace circles on steamed-up
    mirror. I hear my underwater snores and
       stutterings. Dollhouse tableaus vaporize
on loop. Bedside clock with morning sonata.
    Each time when I emerge, memories wash
         lean in the tides—red rover, red rover.

## Redux Suite

*What about your journals—/pages*
*of proof you never changed/ no*
*matter what the mirror tells you.*
                    -Kim Addonizio

When you were 16, you filled a journal page
about your first job—the lingerie department
at Kmart— and how you imagined those black
see-through baby dolls with eenie weenie
red bows pretending they could counter
divorce proceedings. Today with your man
of three decades—clear cold of December,
this overlook above Darby Creek, this elevator
taking you closer to heaven & you are winged,
the *Peter Peter Peter* of two titmice plucking
thin branches that vein cloudy blue. Beat
by beat the have-to want-to push-pull slide
of it, the nagging lacunas—knife to cut bread,
knife to nick my enemy. At Osprey Lake
no osprey but your shoulder far from his
as you stand in solemn rupture beneath
sixty or so turkey vultures, punctuating
the arms of a massive oak as dusk settles
in—next entry to claim you.

## Mama Was a Big Band Singer

I was miniature     at her ankles

       mining the caverns     of her bottom pantry

          economy cans of whole peaches dressed     in *A&P* labels:

   voluptuous melba orbs     with bowtie leaves     & backdrops velvety black

            all balancing a fat scrapbook stuffed with news clippings     8 x 10
glossies.


In her kitchen I swayed cross-legged to the lilt     of her show tunes

                         our family's pre-dinner overture

       she nursing a frying pan of sizzling liver     & onions     *Luck*

           *be a lady tonight*     Lyrics my passport

     to the cosmology     of her heart     *I'll be seeing you*

           bright blouses matching a smorgasbord

      of bejeweled fatties     melodies blooming on her tongue     *Blue skies*

          *smiling at me.*

Late into the nights     when she could no longer longhand her words

    she pecked tender messages     from her script typewriter

       tucked them deep into her cookbooks

  secret harmonies that surprise     then serenade me     a lifetime later.
Late into the nights     when she could no longer longhand her words

    she pecked tender messages     from her script typewriter

       tucked them deep into her cookbooks

  secret harmonies that surprise     then serenade me     a lifetime later.

## Creekside

Last night my mother made treaty with the monster
under my bed. Front yard pine needles nest in my hair

because I won't give up on keeping tally of fireflies.
Mouse pops out of the toaster, magic streaks across

the counter as I grab two squares of butter cake and
stuff them into my backpack. Pink Schwinn, my mustang

that I l ride at odd angles through the neighborhood
or park at the mouth of a path to hike down to harvest

echoes at the toes of waterfall. Today brims with girl
knowledge—my pocket knife, willow whistle, a tattered

library book about Annie Oakley who seems to be west
of everything except this creekside. Her episodes spider

down. She's that handprint in the bark, a birthday action
figure with a string that pulls on legacy.  I want to braid

her an ivy crown, aim her .22 caliber to the sky, sip from
her loving cups. Through breeze, Sitting Bull whispers

his Lakota name for her, *Little Sure Shot* with both eyes
open. Some day I'm going to get me a fancy pair of cowboy

boots but in the meantime I've got to get home.  Late for
casserole, pine needles still jagging my hair, and something

else I won't give up on, the palindrome of my mother's
chest scars, targets where her breasts used to be.

## Dear Sandwiches

In order to feed this story
with a bounty of picnic fillings
I took to skipping my way through
insurance sandwiches, tipping
the scales between
overmuch and under.
Everyone is usually more pleasing
in the kitchen so we became troubadours
in alchemy so to speak.
When baby sandwich grew its teeth
in the cupboard, parents got used to sucking
on dormant keys & pacifiers like sardines,
gherkins, maraschino cherries.
Hope was the aroma of onions frying.
Savory tears complicated lunch.
Chew chew chew not always enough.
Rusty keys in a jar.
Mistresses on mattresses.
Crumbs on chipped plates & globs
of bargain white bread stuck
onto the roof of his mouth.

## Surrealistic Pillow

So many pink plush pillows huddle atop my
canopy bed, me at 15 gazing at Grace Slick—
lithe & just ever-so-cool on her album cover.

Why can't soup cans command my frizzled
locks to look like hers, coquette bangs upstaging
every one of her sexy bandmates.  Down my street,

Jehovah Witness kindergarteners wait for me to feed
them slices of cold roast while their parents flee to
another church meeting but I've got ten more minutes

to blast "White Rabbit" from my powder blue record
player that's like a petite suitcase packed with psychedelic
lyrics.  I know what *surrealistic* means now because

I've highlighted it on page 1367 of my desk dictionary
& that term also seems to apply to the Watchtower pamphlets
that their mother will send home with me this evening when

I will crumple them into my parka's deep pocket, along
with two perfumed dollar bills, & mutter at her front
door on a snowy school night a plucky— *Go ask Alice.*

*The most important thing*
      *is that everyone who wants a catapult gets a catapult.*

(*J. Olien's cartoon caption in The New Yorker, April 15, 2019*)

Last week my son married a pretzel but never told me, me
      who avoids Facebook at her own peril, peril now
his of too many posted puns salting salty declarations of love
      for the bread knots knotting their union, bioavailable
of course. A full course of flirty ukulele melodies,
      mellowing the launch of any pretzel wife
         in a wiffery state of affection which could catapult
her catapult which will hurl him as an easy mark—
      mark my words—his vulnerability made the best angle
         angling her battle machine for tendering
his tenderness baked through.  Together their selfies
      selfisized their physics—she the cuddling counterweight
for his payload loaded for romance & just the right smack—
      then *snack*—his snack with a late late night beer.

## Her Cats

Here's to us— her troika
of feline sisters, our
days a button jar of

naps. Strays we are
arbitrators of our own
plots:  Black Persian

boyish & coy; Calico
a camisole in a larynx;
Tortie defiant & cynical,

broken from another home.
She's the straight player who
sets up our catitude for

canned pea juice, tampon
string toys, reruns of *My
Cat From Hell.*

She wonders how we roam
our forests of thoughts. We,
geometry of goddesses

worthy of Chekov, Alvarez
& Autsin; cat lives lived
more honestly than hers.

## Titling My Husband's New Painting

Take me along when color
forgets itself, an interval
with no duration, the vibrant
hush as hues abide, your
cutting edge of practice.
Hover me above canvas
when instinct remembers
forgetfulness, the peg
of moment vanishes, &
fog of knowing clears.
Our steaming mugs
of morning coffee
toast what we have
come to say to each
other, but then plot
exhales & it's that
traceless trace
when stubborn ghosts
of what has slipped
our minds   appears.

# Miss McGlaughlin and the Road to Marvel

*The octopus houses three hearts* as we
      placed our fifth grade palms over ours.
After *I pledge allegiance to the flag:*
      *Travelers, how will we seize today?*
Order in the cloak room, our cubbies
      obedient altars to rain boots, parkas,
mittens with clips—manifold of parental
      coddling, but Miss McGlaughlin pointed
our way to trumpeting joy of elephants
      & pomegranate hearts full of jewels.
The desk globe, her orb of dazzle, &
      a punch bowl brimming with postcards
each carrying a story from three decades
      of adventure. Cardinal—her winter courier
at the raised window, & on the turtle's back
      secret messages if we squinted long
enough. Our months studying art &
      mythology but really how to be a deep
sea diver—what do Van Gogh's brushstrokes
      whisper, what does the invention of muses
show us about the Ancients? Class trips
      to her farm of peacocks, llamas & renegade
sunflower fields, tails of back road dust
      dancing behind our marigold bus.
Ida McGlauglin, know your frog eyes,
      bobblehead, & cartoon dresses still
belong to a gangly girl you taught
      to freight with windows wide open.

## Ode to Time Travel

History likes to fluctuate between catastrophic destruction
        and messianic redemption, but lives mostly in between,
Yahweh, our most treasured literary device as we begin
        our dying right there in the womb where *vowels*
get invented, and then how it goes, that subsoil of childhood,
        tiny ballerina twirling in my jewelry box and me
tilting my head towards my mother's fossilized whispers, *it's*
        *okay this keepsake was made in Germany but no Jewish*
*daughter of mine will be going there as a foreign exchange student,*
        and long matchsticks as ghost soldiers proffered at our family
fireplace, my father squatting on an antique birthing chair as he stokes
        flames somewhere up the road to Homewood, plus more places
that can't be measured by maps or miles but by windows and mirrors
        that would give us a second chance if only we could return,
lobbed through thick clouds of silence, and the sister/brother pair
        of kittens that vibrate at my neck to cure me of my sadness
for a troubled son fading away, his dark future I ache to revise,
        now drawn in an archer's bow of geese launching
my backyard ravine up to its cold, grey November morning.

## Yellow Comes and Goes As It Pleases

Someday I may learn my lemons,
resist the marigold's musky dirge,
for I have this man who drags his feet

through piles of rotting banana peels,
residue of strict smoothies too thick
for punchlines. Too often he trudges back

into the dark forest with ocher pigment
smudged on his forehead and cheeks to
hunt for old stumps that he kicks over so that

yellowjackets swarm and tether. Yet, I have
seen his gentle palm cradling corn kernels
for backyard goldfinches and receive loving

texts that he types with his toes while curling, in his
kitchen home gym, a pair of sun-kissed dumbbells.

## Ouroboros

I could purse
my lips no longer
instead I opened my maw
to swallow the coins
of his small numbers
& the bristles
of his retractable tape.
His nourishment tasted
wrong & eventually I spit
the seeds back
exhaled all swoon &
hissed to that first day
that grew this last.
As I stood at his shrine
I felt his slow slink
beneath my soles
then tilted
my new
summer hat.

## Clothes Horse

You like wearing a soup of polka dots with rascally pockets
        and that hat of ostrich-egg-over-easy. You're a landscape
seen through pinhole, born for knowing how to keep your clothes
        dancing. Passersby nod through clouds around you,
gardenia with a bit of ginger on top.  Sometimes you're in the habit
        of spandex, buttery soft camel toe whispering for guests.
Sometimes you're all in for the dissenting swag of a judge's collar.
        But always you're hungry for the click & collect, or thrifting
in the hunt for your next highlight reel. Closets never enough,
        scarves and gloves and bracelets color-sorted in the pantry.
You tell us it was the shapeshifting of adolescence that got you here,
        the scripture of accessory, the rebel arithmetic of your
outsiderness + your outside-ness = bondage trousers, chain mail nose
        ring, neon spikes for hair.  Now it's martingale back and designer
pouch with teacup pooch.  You say you always wear your soul on
        your sleeve, your style slippery or stonewashed. And there you
go again, chiffon creature preening in limelight,  combat boots prancing
        for romantic notions like *sprezzatura* and *je ne sais quoi.*

## At the Fashion Museum

The covenant we cast since
days of fig leaf & loincloth,
thrill of what's under the zipper,
silk stripped against an ear of corn.
Enter this frozen farm of mannequins
with phantom antlers & rooster
combs. Gallery corrals where craft
is high, fruits hang low & bucketfuls
of hue know how to color an empire.

Defying brittle sepia tones of
history with spinning jenny like
a noble dinosaur with its offspring—
wool frocks, cotton petticoats,
gingham coy & lace demure, teasing
tulle, taffeta, cashmere, tooth of
hound, & buds of lavender pregnant
with the grammar of ornament.

Fashion, the great sartorial pollinator—
nipple windows, suits that speak
louder than words, hands swallowed
by sleeves, youthquake of ready-to-wear.
To reimagine pleats or gender binary,
orange as new pink, snow globes
of counter-culture couture.

Temple where we worship
the language of fabric & dismiss
ghosts of expiration dates.

## An Almost Ghazal For My Mother's Hats

A memory fermata from my brother's musty
basement—your weathered cache of dormant hats.

Who wants to be a milliner?  It's me who yearns to
adorn you again with your signature crown panache.

Not Carmen Miranda's tutti frutti tower or the
mystique that Audrey Hepburn's brims begat

but your astute and effortless pillbox, satin
cream to match your linen dress, jeweled flats.

Not in Lady Gaga's floppy blushpink Boho
or in Schiaparelli's high-heeled shoe-hat

but your quail-feathered bowler with emerald ribbon—
pure hattitude for luncheons, their green-eyed chitchat.

When you stepped out you were a standout, behold
that black-velvet, pearl-beaded, mink-trimmed half-hat,

your summer straw with gingham flowers, a tufty
clown bouncing on the headband of your circus hat.

Tonight I salvage from sagging round boxes
your weathered cache of trademark hats, still

beguiled by scarlet lips, veiled fascinators, this daughter's
finishing school for accessorizing—the play in being all that.

## Stetson

You've made a name for yourself, a lifetime
sheltering heads from the aloof of stars.
In your ribbon band still nests a dime novel
& season tickets to all you can eat spaghetti westerns.
Addicted to the notion of legacy, you hunger
for emoji status, boss of the plains, desperado
on horseback atop a silver saddle.
From sentimental pools of childhood, I never
was a chocolate box heroine but a high-crowned,
neckerchiefed badlander roaming manicured
suburban sidewalks on a piebald bronco,
my fat-tired Schwinn. They say Custer died
in his calvary-creased Stetson. My Annie Oakley
knock-off from the local Kmart suited me just fine.
Whistling to the rhythm of hoofbeats tucked
under my brim, I squinted at tenderfoots tossing
their baseballs, my bare-boned *yups* & *nopes*
at the dinner table, mama's lasagna never as good
as campfire beans. So I didn't use you to slap a steer,
smother grass fires, or serve as a target in gunfights,
but you were my gateway to the unbridled joy
of playing out my world theatrically. How
illiterate I was of ways to endure a hard land.

## "Spring Fashion Modeled by Rising Young Poets"

*O* (The Oprah Magazine)

Stock the shelves with shrink
wrapped metaphors. The Poetnistas
are here. Each pronounced a connoisseur,
cherry-picked from the stacks. Each packaged,
full-paged and ankle deep
in her very own reflecting pool.
What eight goddesses who write poems
are wearing.

She Verbs now She Nouns.
Their verses pervert into accessory, sink
into sand, stretch across a megaphoned
hard-on, are knifed and forked
on a porcelain plate. *Her zen minimal is*
*channeled through the clean lines of*
*a French-cuffed shirt. The teal,*
*peach and chartreuse of a pencil*
*skirt and sequined cardigan make*
*her feel va-va-va voom.*

Frame us, too, salacious
window lickers fit for a fitting
room where beatnik turtlenecks
and black toreador pants hang
whimpering on another clever hook
of commodity.

## Wrists

We like to adorn them with
columns of rhyming bangles
to tease out tender murmurs
of pulse. With confident cufflinks,
clockwork of too many complications,
ruffles for uselessness, astrological
tattooes—all charms for our most narrow
but not enough to forgive deep
histories of handcuff & shackle.
Delicate body part for
lacey bridal gloves,
archer's sheath,
baby's protector
from droplets too hot.
Deep histories
of handcuff & shackles,
never enough to forgive—
charms of our most narrow
those wrists rhyming
with bracelets to tease out
murmurs of pulse.

## Catwalk

Remember when we chewed
fat off hides, stitched with
sinew, Neanderthal fashion?

Now shimmering animals
swivel with uncomfortable
charm—flanked by

flourish, vehicle for
reverie as their heels
click across the trill

of runway. Leg gears
pump a parade of
sleepwalkers, arms

like clock weights,
torsos delivering
ideas that thrive on

sashay.  Pose
mascara-heavy,
more dry martini

than mineral water,
armature with span
of hanger—hot

pepper jam &
jelly of bitchfest.

## Her Self Portrait at Saks

Coat those designer jeans

in the languages of vogue

& obscenity of price tag

paint splats & whiskered thighs counterfeit
        ::studio lofts
        ::cotton fields
        ::Bavarian immigrant with coal mine cure all

NOW dust-brown stains can't bear sneakers

        that blind with their whiteness

            the metrics when skeevy

                calculates the warp & the weft

                    of commerce

                            button fly
        boot cut
                or bumster

        plumb tuckered out      before she charges them

# His Way Was To

*for Lee Alexander McQueen (1969-2010)*

winnow through the cut, armadillos to anchor
bold fruit & smirk's purity.  He cinched with a final
belt the knot of his notable, fragile buccaneer's
scent still nesting in the hides of his dogs.
Long live alien stilettos, shoulder beaks,
blood sighing beneath beaded tattoos.
Tight tight corseted bravado, far-from-fine
lace, the asymmetrical & the ravaged all luxed
for live performance. Opera in the next sequined
dress tarnished & distressed. Couture his anti-thesis,
sullen wings sprouted after a lost mother, his last
note blooming on a weary copy of *The Descent
of Man* fringed with orphaned threads, his riddle
for the bite & the bruise.

## How to be a Maven

*Color can raise the dead.* -Iris Apfel

Call yourself an *accidental* icon,
which is as far as a life of affluence
can shed its fortuitous self. Make
sure your Barbie doll doppelgänger
misplaces all your wrinkles & your
black rims of flying saucer eyebobs
avert weathered years. Museum &
Commerce with a capital C will come
calling to stroke the conspicuous layers
of exotic prerogatives which were
always just you. Mixing high & low,
you ain't no badass fad, just a lifetime
of making your way towards a century
at the altar of freewheeling surprise.

## Did Icon

Did Versace billow beyond stilettos sky-highed
with peep-toed platforms triggered.
Did Balenziaga four-side a cocktail dress,
Armani rebirth old Hollywood, mused
by mini-dress metal.
Did red snake & crocodile scales lavish operatic for
Dolce Gabbana massimalismo,
fabulous by the water with champagne flutes.
Did flirty hip-high split ruffle-&-tulle frothy,
delicate pastry tasty with semi-shear pleats.
Did von Furstenberg slink the wrapped jersey so comfortable
no underwear, so comfortable get laid.
Did bubble silhouettes lampshade hems,
paint-by-numbers walk as perfume atomizers.
Did tulip fields loosen with free-flowing hair,
bloom surreal sweater sets, pussy bowtie all blouses in sight.
Did Gucci risque' hippie chic & coquette a pout.
Did folds light-as-air float a train, make us want to tango,
orgasm with winks.
Did scarlet beret ravish its sequins like a great clarifier,
safety pins oversized strategized flesh.
Did raw beef bypass butcher,
a rooster feather a headdress to scold award shows.
Did pink wool suit & matching pillbox
scar an America alongside couture alabaster
ballooning above a sidewalk grate.
Did Gucci's blackface jumper,
H&M's *coolest monkey in the jungle,*
& Burberry's hoodie with strings tied like a noose
expose abscessed fangs.

## Lineage

This first story, this chin of fire, this Sun and its daughters, primordial mirror.
The aproned goddess returns, fondles the crosspoints where warp and weft conjoin,
      reclaims shards of ocean turquoise, phoenix flames.
Ocher medallion looms large, epitaph for each master who crushed then transformed
        mineral, insect, shellfish.  For Queen Liliuokalani, the sisters of Gee's Bend,
these threads bear the needle's prayer fired through the eyes of every woman's weaving.
                Quilt, poised and illuminated,
                    another resurrection
                    in the politics of textile.

# Ginger Rogers' Feathered Gown

mothballs don't suit me
        and I probably deserve hell
    ostriches plucked        bloody and raw
yet if you squint beyond the celluloid
      gently I will lift you
    onto an aqua cloud
        and Fred will evaporate
while you float    with me
        and Ginger
          a swan seduced
   spinning like sugar

      shimmering across white satin

    imagine your cheek

       caressed by my tender plumage

  I will dip you

    into honeyed meringue

        I will make you

          surrender to divinity

    I am the dress that will survive you all

## Yellow Dress

for Suzy Bishop
from Wes Anderson's *Moonrise Kingdom*

How many stories can live inside your story?
To move forward by branching out—matchstick

quilting of inhale, exhale, inhale of a runaway girl
with teal eyelids, withering stare and outbursts

that stalk you in the jungle of adolescence.
Your lemon sweet suitcase with contraband

library books & binoculars that keep you peeled
to preserve magic in distance.  How many

trick-or-treat girls will match themselves
to your coral mini, your perky knee socks,

your raven in a welter with saddle-shoed talons.
Seaside, a geeky beau nestles daisies in your hair.

His emerald beetles, skewered by fishhooks,
dance at your earlobes to match the confection

of your training bra & print panties—a timid rumba
to the smoky lilt of a '60s French songbird.

He so gets you & you him—he'll be your lightning
rod when the opera of biblical hurricane rips through.

Behold, little match girl who rewrites her own story.
Safety you learn comes from the world resting

atop a generous turtle and a yellow dress matching
sun-bleached walls of your bay window perch.

## Primer for a Press Conference Wardrobe

Consonant for arrogance be a credit to your cape.
Who will lick the sores of your Achilles heels,

a skinhead's 18-hole boot shorthand for aggression.
Whether patriotic ties like petrified lava

or scarfed bucketfuls of Matisse, laden
your muddy soles with mission, 26 bones

for 270 million steps. Freeze dry inside those
capsule suits a tardy recognition. Dominate

the room like a glitter gown, firecrackers round your
pointing fingers, kitten heels to kick the hungry cats.

## What Fancied Her

If a toilet seat can be a lyre & applause stored in a box
then this is the story of a believer: your closet in the
candy-colored language of clown—you with a pimiento
center & comfortable as a sock,  never ruffled or lacy
but blooming in tie-dye spider spin or echoes of mandarin
fish—you were red-rubber-nose elated to be here, up on
your toes for Bird's Nest sandals you bartered in
Mongolia—crowned in a polka dotted bowler from
Milan—at your fingertips a turquoise ukulele busked
for a decade at Carnival Madrid. Then, for your funeral—
when black could have absorbed everything—we schemed
to gather dressed as White Face or  Auguste, your ashes
like apostle plant petals flowered the threads
of a lake that for a lifetime loved you back.

## Well Shod

They gentrify the old West with python & ostrich
or click the homesick heels of ruby, the lazy
slip-on slip-off of loafers, inventions of slogans pithy—
*moon shoes: mini trampolines for your tootsies.* My father's
army of polished Florsheim nines line up in his closet
in his closet like an obedient narrow-sized parade, my new
daisy Kmart sandals for flirty cheese fries on opening day
of the fair, splotches of chocolate milkshake assault
my saddled oxfords which in turn deliver a bruise
(the size of a coconut) on the mean bitch shin of schoolmate,
negative heels only make campus hills steeper but college
boyfriend's blue suede shoes make me fall in love for a lifetime,
I ain't no dominatrix but I know how to work thigh-high boots
intimate as skin, then tibial tendon surgery cause my stilettos
to mutiny. Arrogance of jeweled soles that patronize others
to manipulate their bootstraps, how to shoe the world, dominance
of Air Jordans dangle from a power line, at the sit-in we throw
frenzied sneakers at the mayor, too many screenshots of her
Jimmy Choos but not worse than those evil stepsisters cutting
off their heel or toes. Gibran believed that the earth is always
jazzed whenever it feels our soles bare but we also stand tall
in shoes that resemble buildings, armadillos, or handcrafted
in the wee hours by elves. Wear dreams on your feet my
mother cooed, dew-sprinkled sprigs of rosemary and thyme
tucked overnight under tongues.

# When Matryoshka Dolls Take the Runway

*Like the Morton salt girl, they never wavered from a belief in infinite regression. Thou shalt covet the trajectory of babushka. On the shore of the Volga, past daydreams of Venetian blinds, a pair of silk stockings with tender black seams curled through forest branches luring woodcutters from their benches. Finally they settled around the neck of a rooster girl like a timid scarf with a broom & basket thesis. It was then that the Matryoshka dolls ripened into their universe:*

When the Matryoshka dolls take the runway
they whirl to Stravinsky's *The Rite of Spring* & cup the borders of empty—
dream of gauzy negligees, saucy slippers & catwalks carpeted with hay—
nest robin eggs from government corruption—
beckon endangered leopards to drink slowly from their halves

When the Matryoshka dolls take the runway
they masquerade as spice jars—
pose as proletariats in the pantry—
shimmy over Twiggish waifs while chanting fertility spells

When the Matryoshka dolls take the runway
their long black lashes launch like butterflies working attitude
as they wear folktale embroideries of magic rubles, sacred valleys

When the Matryoshka dolls take the runway
it is their red of reds that hums the hum      how easily we hide in one another.

# American Shop Windows

*after "The Munich Mannequins" by Sylvia Plath*

*Mannequins lean tonight*
sober-faced giraffes,

eyebrow apparitions, torsos
imagining animal pleasures.

Surrogate armies defend
molded nipples & navels,

postural idiosyncrasies
always captured ready

to wear. Tweens with their
own rod & base, trail through

the mall, libidos with fables
glittering from cellphones.

Smoothies sustain them.
Credit cards explain them.

Suburban world trips the axis.
Selfies, like flatlined cameos

frame vapor tongues numb
under fluorescence.

## Sweatpants Theology

Lost reasons to dress up.
Quarantine a voodoo temple.
Crows fly over cities, towns, centuries.
Silhouettes loom across the chessboard
and words can't seem to go any further.
Mystery plays perform in cardboard theaters
this time with masks and hospital ships.
Homebody sweatpants have a mind of their own
one leg then the other, slogan t-shirts with sweat
stains, a new state of merch.
Stumble through reverberating chatter,
surplus of molecular metaphor,
publicized publicized connotation.
Pivot on how little can be enough
to take the long view.

## Buttonhole

The upholstery for our nakedness
knows all our bodies' lies—
what's draped, untucked,
or buttoned up like kudzu.
We have been fasteners
for thousands of years,
our provenance for connection.

Peculiar norms thrive.
Gendered buttons still a thing—
right for men, left for women,
holes that push liberal
buttons.  How to summon
each clotheshorse to press
the red button
on a global fashion
to fast & furious.

This buttonhole
we squeeze through—
a ravishing that ravages,
high crimes committed
in too-ready-to-wear,
tyranny of quarterly returns
embedded into bent-over shoulders
from Manchester to Rana Plaza.

What should we wear today?
Frog loops too loose
to button down white noise
of sweatshop—lint & fibers
clinging to too many nose hairs.
Jacket pockets fill with
stones the size of baby
potatoes, hoarse yawps limp
across too many landscapes.

## Mermaid Envy

Especially with my tail
when I go like this and weave
through chilled murmurs
of deep to call you, you
marvel at my kind.
My tongue, primordial red,
my long long rainbow hair,
all invisible in inky darkness
where color and imagination abides.
I don't think about
being charming even with
what you call my marble eyes,
translucent refugees from
ancient calculating machines
wedged into underwater caverns
of my shipwreck bounty.
Islands are the middles of my stories.
Sun squints.
Moon opens its mouth.
Ocean is sound.
All necessary things.

## Faye Takes a Breath

Launched from the lake's muzzle
      your bones swirl
in amniotic womanhood
        against the undertow of adolescence.

Your face a full moon & you take
        breath,  exhale flocks of dragonflies
& golden tadpoles, swallow
      old stories, deep song.

In time you will claim río debajo del rio
        your river beneath the river—
your hair blonde kelp,  no life
      jacket or bow line

you are nimble,
      a vernal shapeshifter
treading waters
      of kith & kin.

Necklaces ripple 'round you,
      your sultry appointments with the world
may embrace fluidity—a she, a he,
      a them, each to each.  You raise

your arms above your head
      then submerge—
Anaïs Nin tattooed onto each wrist,
      gift from your mother:

on left— *I must be a mermaid,*
      on right—*I have no fear of depths*
*and a great fear*
      *of shallow living.*

## Two Windows

after *Heat Wave* by Nadir Nelson and
*Young Woman At a Window* by Salvador Dali

Forearms of two young women anchor
each onto their window sills of launchpad.

Rainbow cool of what can be licked from a stick.
Chaste harmony in drapery folding with a back's melody.

Cheekbones and cleavage glisten in the heat,
goddess chin erect in the sidewise glory of heiroglyph.

Relaxed shoulders, tilting hip, ankle coyly pressed
against its other, a face the ocean's possession.

These daughters own their gazes, challenge yours,
their futures there for their taking.

## Weekend Tectonic

The raw and marbled pork shoulder lay bare on the table
        so she rested her shoulder against it.
Her mother's crusty plates schemed in the sink while
        legions of ants pillaged a half-eaten cruller.

She didn't know what *haphazard* meant
        or even *meekly* but at the laptop
she dutifully began to answer vocabulary questions
        & mused as an 8th grade girl can—
        if only life could be multiple choice
        & if only the fourth try counted.

She was at the edge of wilderness in this kitchen,
        a student of the flavors of geyser.
        A fly straddled *X* on her keyboard,
        a pair of wine glasses with snapped necks
            surrendered on the counter.

That night she dreamed of a mass of orphaned balloons
        huddling together in a corner of the cosmos.
Next morning, when she opened her eyes
        she felt knotted but akin
        to the period at the end of a sentence.

Downstairs her mother was finishing her mug
        of clumsy imperative.
She was plum out of dazzle, & her shift
        at Denny's was waiting.

How to right what's wrong with a life—
        with a nail gun or a prayer?
*How many times do I have to tell you*
        as magma heaved upward
        & finally their two continents
        cleaved for a lifetime.

## Double Vanitas

*...I felt like Oppenheimer or something. What have I done?*
*Because it's going to need high security all its life.*
Damien Hirst on his artwork, For the Love of God

Our god is uncanny, pixelated
in its effigy antics, elated for

this shimmering, crusted skull—
8,601 flawless diamonds and a

pear-shaped pink one, third
eye of the forehead, technical

refinement by hired hands.
A concept is a concept is a

commodity. On a dare, our god forged
toothy marketplace of forbidden

fruit. No one to blame.
God's way to animate

another exquisite corpse
for our laps, each gem-stud

making its claim for punchline.
Platinum cast of a lucky 18th

century chap who got to keep
his teeth that held a pipe, chewed

on penny loaf. Hollow man
immortalized by hollow man for

50 million pounds in auction.
Our god smirks behind a two-way

mirror, slow time holds us
in the drop jaw of still life.

Luminous decay, market shelves
bloated, overripe and spoiling.

## Umbrella Man (1998)

*for Peter Max*

Headless with Magritte bowler
your painting echoes in a stranger's voice
now the man is teetering
through puddles & rainbows
light dimming
color at your back
Buddhists say *mind has no color*
your wife erases herself from the world
others skin for your nectar
the gods are leaving you
but thunder will remain soft in our ears.

## Clown Suite

What beckons beyond ringmaster— our countenance,
display board for algorithms that live outside
space & time, our arms and legs so damn irresponsible,

our eyebrows are Morse code for mischief & mayhem.
We are refugees sired by Victorian ghosts, cartoonify
communion masks that refuse to behave.  Our color

commentary teeters between folly & fear. Tasty eggs
on our faces, cushiony hearts on sleeves and Sisyphus
garlands around our necks.  Mics drop like flies.

In our prop rooms of concepts, plastic spoons dillydally
in honey jars and tongues gain a toehold.  Phonetic
proximity is fodder: address, no undress the audience!

Entrees ferment in petri dishes while we tune tiny
fiddles to squeaking bouquets of balloons.  To slap
or be slapped, to fractal expected order, to turn inside

out that religion of toying. We are funhouse companions
for high-minded and rococo jugglers. Our history is potted,
our corpus abundant, we vault and caper without any bones.

Our smirks are blood-red, summaries of gravity's ad lib,
We are pop-up disciples who summon cuckoo-clock birds
from our trousers, officiate funerals for mosquitos that

we adored. We bang on the ground to make it sound
hollow, catch hurling dinner plates behind our backs—
we are crafty and clingy and closer to God than you think.

## Emily May Be Weary

of surviving as a ventriloquist Sphinx
for novelists, filmmakers, memelords
—& poets like me.  Spectrographic
erasures bloom with threadbare

secrets—Snapchat daguerreotypes
in 3D flurries of foxglove crowns—
posters & t-shirts dwell in too much
possibility, while her jasmine tea blend

boasts to rival sunset in a cup.
How fresh can brandy black cake
taste in the rewind of how-to-videos
or namesake ice cream flavors prevail

in the melting? Like her herbarium,
collected & pressed dry—Emily's
riddles may tire—rickety dialogue
slanting between spirit & dust.

# Lunatics in Ohio

*Athens Lunatic Asylum (1874-1993)*

They buttered judgment, county physicians and judges—
insanity, a slippery cat.  By horse or wagon or through
the dusty rowdiness of small- town train depot, patients
transpired.  Some with family, some in straitjackets—
how to decipher a Victorian rubric overlooking the Hocking
Valley where the glacier finally stopped—a healing temple
with drifts of magenta flower heads and Adena ghosts.

Imagine so many protagonists at windows with mandala grills,
moths nibble in closets, grand fountain harbors a summer
alligator—powerful muscle with beach glass eyes. Spoons
wander in bowls of mutton stew, chrysanthemums prideful
in the greenhouse, outings at a natural spring, violins
in the ballroom, then sleep in wings where clocks keep
watch over the musk of sorrow, cotton of surrender.

Ancestor squirrels still stir these thick woods, turkey vultures
nest in weathered eaves, stone wall here, old apple tree there,
dusty casebooks with footprints of enrolled sufferers—
chaotic mixture of epileptics, discarded elders with dementia,
shell-shocked soldiers, tramps as nuisance, violent criminals,
mothers with menstrual derangement, chronic masturbators,
defeated suiciders who aimed at hanging or swallowed pins.

Some say phantoms roam these decaying halls and the cemetery
of weary headstones, many bearing lone ID numbers.
On the floor of an upstairs room, the stain of a woman's corpse
evaporates and returns. Imagine the mounting stigma
of overcrowding, experiments in electroshock, freezing
water baths, lobotomies with ice picks—to not forget
almost a century of jacks-in-the-box, stuffed in tightly
with trembling tally marks on their walls.

# Between the lashes of [their] eyes*

*[He] was the Cecil B. DeMille of circus photography.*
from *Step Right This Way: The Photographs of Edward J. Kelty*

Take out your magnifying glass and relish
the gritty confections of this coffee table book.
Poof of flash powder—each circus congress
in large format and wide angle, posed linear
and otherworldly, what a class picture sets
its heart on—crowded bodies, each face casting
its noble imprint, some arms making prayers
around another's shoulders, all dismissing
any sky. Elephant handlers with their whips and
flourishes, candy butchers and showgirls with ostrich-
feathered fannies, teeterboard tumblers, ticket takers,
tattooed sword swallowers, tightrope daredevils, piles
of elaborate clowns, and all the gaudy deformities of
sideshow citizens. As they stand there, imagine
their memories of mothers, crumpled Tarot cards
in back pockets, perfumes and spices nestled into
costumes, onions and grease and the burn of whiskey
on their breath. The earth turns and they still give
way to copies of themselves, muscular and boastful
under hats and headdresses and fresh from the fervor
of sequined matinee. Poof of flash powder—
they all trusted his box's eye for a future where they
would be lost yet harvested now in black & white
wonder cabinets where we can't get enough of looking.

*Walt Whitman, *Leaves of Grass*

## Circus Lullaby

You my drifting cloud   dream again of your axis mundi high wire
your calliope     your nursing cousins Miss Melody & Miss Cacophony
Hush   Hush   there's too much    still too much exhaling
from your life-sized posters peeling    tall & tattered on fences & barns
Octaves of ideas    sired by dime novels &   run    away
wishes curling at supper tables in Zanesville & Chillicothe
Memories peep    through a paper hoop    elephants sashay
on revolving cabinet cards       nonsense bruises clown car
upholstery      whips of lion tamers slither through sawdust
Now deride distance        from mud show pageant    tweeze
clarity from sideshow angels       Hush      Hush   Miss Bareback
dream beyond       your launch sideways      dream beyond
the final       striking       of the tent

## P.T. Barnum Drags His Feet

The shopping mall is set adrift,
the iris eye of its camera tightening shut.
Phineas continues to survey
with a mustachioed realtor
another withering funhouse
where mirrors mattered and jumbo
hot dogs ruled the food court.

The empty mouth of a behemoth parking lot
suffers canker sores.  Once brash and elbowy,
the edges of lit corridors now fray and
fringe.   Big boxes dark. Phineas.drags
his feet across a pocked emporium.
Cotton candy in his teeth, he pisses into
a grimy urinal. His pulse skitters.
Is this a terrible mistake, or a case
of playing dead.  Phantoms linger—
fuckwild teenagers, perfume samples,
corporate black magic.

How can we keep what we can't sustain.
Common sparrows lace
its chain link fence, field mice
gnaw its drywall. Phineas chews
on his Regius Double Corona.
Someone will turn off the lights,
demall another American museum
of its curiosities while in the ether
sideshows bark algorithms into fingertips
and bears still dance for bread.

## Beyond Sliced Bread, The Greatest Things Since

sliced rhymes experimented with chronology,
sliced seduction unearthed droplets of memory,
sliced broths of autobiography roiled its geometry,
sliced soap bubbles translated the alchemy of chatter.
These greatest things since sliced syntax made semantics
more digestible, sliced applause bootlegged vanity, sliced
angels mapped humanity's greasy fingerprints, and sliced
foxholes filled their baskets to capacity.  Hail the greatest
things since sliced innocence vaporized melodies
encyclopedic, sliced archives ferreted out crowns
of gumption, sliced magic framed the rationale of riffing,
sliced malaprop invented the truce of echoes.  Seek holy
grail of greatest things since sliced decisions tattooed
the stars with abandon, sliced effervescence edged
the edges of comprehension, sliced prayers massaged
the algorithm's rictus, sliced wonder surpassed
thresholds of no deposit no return.

# Calculus of Showman

*I don't care what the newspapers say about me
as long as they spell my name right.*
                                    —P. T. Barnum

The underbelly of any lie is imagination
and the footprints of self-made legend
can still be forgery a century later
in the candy-appled prances of splashy
musicals with amusable jazz hands.

P.T. Barnum, the dangler of trite and trope,
his narratives circled the rails as circus trains
steamed through firmament and valleys,
the ferocity of humbug cornered its America
into itinerant culture, animal crackers in a box.

Spectacles cast their siren songs—
man became monkey in the skin of another,
tiniest general reared under glass,
public autopsy of her 161-year-old body
opened to the moon.

Erasure, O, Prometheus—
your mortals on exhibit
breathing stale air of cul-de-sac,
their shapes evaporating
leaving polished shadows,
curiosities that signified and served.

Today they are long silenced in translation
yoked in myth and museum—
showman still struts and preens
balancing on their weathered backs.

When did they stretch out in summer fields
to trace faces in the clouds,
wipe their chins shining with peach nectar,
stroll through tender threads of their own weaving.

## Secure Your Ingredients

Press your ear to the side of your refrigerator
      take stock of its raillery
Be the greatest tapaist composing tercets of fried eel skins
      and squid sauce tattoos
Be patient when your cheese wheel pontificates
Let fairies savor episodes of overturned milk
Crush your empty egg shells before a witch boats them out to sea
      with yokes yelping runny off-color jokes
Plant your melon seeds wearing a chiffon negligee under moonlight
Let your cabbage leaves ferment in your purse

Shepherd fogs of much gin tonic
Give your atomic snacks eyes more magicker than spies'
Cry enough tears to dissolve the spilled salt of inertia
Slice the baguette through its hollow heart
      cup your hands for its resurrection
Trust that the wishbone's long leg will detonate the petard
      and release all your crud in your cupboards

Don't cut your noodle before serving
      or scatter your bean in dark corners
Pluck every renegade rice pellet or they will equal
      each zit on your ass
Strum potato roots  to sentimentalize fast food diasporas
Let much meringue will be your Morse code
      French toast your riposte
Take your oath with a necktie of garlic
      and sympathize with that ball of polenta
      wobbling on skewer legs like an egret too drunk
      for a tablecloth snare.

## Day After

*for Sandy Scheur (1949-May 4, 1970)*

Before high school homeroom
as I slide the black arm band
over my bicep I remember
slices of what I knew of you:

in the cafeteria a half-eaten
grilled cheese with your army
of half moons claiming its
triangle of bread—

in civics class the waving
of your palm for the clean
target you made of each question—

in the hallway showcase
the beam of your grin
pronouncing where you were
destined for a first year of college.

This morning you are a distant
schoolmate, one-year ahead
but now a ghost
      wish—if you
hadn't walked to class, stepped
into M1 crossfire, stained ground
with your jugular's flow
became another memorial
for sacrifice biblical & bought.

## Around Our Corner

*At 6:23 a.m. 11-year-old Lizzie Robertson-Rutland*
*was hit by one vehicle then another as she tried*
*to cross the street to her school's bus stop.*

How many tears can pink
Mylar hearts hold
fluttering from the utility pole
that witnessed your murder.

How can we spool you
back, press a blunt stylus
into a sheet of acetate
then lift your double
collision from the world.

Eyes tight fisted
we see your bowels
        bust into your chest,
your spleen & heart
            rupture,
        ribcage shatter
                & flood,

perfumed stillness of your princess
        t-shirt,          spinning of your
        unicorn earrings,        skewed
    lullaby of red dawn
            flashing,  compressed
        syntax of
                hit & run.

## Titan Moving Out

Every elliptical orbit that binds sons
to fathers moves with the eccentrics
of time-reckoning.  Father Saturn
says you're moving out—
his favorite moon doesn't seem
to need his papa's ringlets anymore.
So far you're the only body
besides Earth with surfaces
that sire rivers, lakes, deep seas.
Cue your Titan brethren who launched
the ancient craft of stealing fire,
the vault of heavens pressing
down on rebellious shoulders.
You're big enough to bully
Mercury, and now you're pulling
away from home four inches a year.

Some say with wings strapped
to our arms we could fly
your cloud-filled skies
with no more effort than walking.
We aim our backyard telescopes
for haiku snapshots of you.

Dragonfly will visit—
the NASA drone calibrated
to probe your impact crater
slammed ten millennia ago,
to measure your frigid ways.
Free-range scientists yearn
to tilt impossible spheres
and find another place
where ingredients
for life may live.
But you are an old god,
a distant machine
stubborn and likely
to keep
your secrets
close.

## Once Upon a Time Sestina

She grows hollow like a gilded castle but her will remains, naked and wild.
She knows how to frame the moon then eat its margins.
Often, she folds myths into postcards and mails them to subjects.
*What use is the dancing* she asks herself when twilight settles in.
In the tower she unfurls a map of her beloveds, circling each state of ache.
Her garden gnomes pace the skin of moat, taking inventory of where lost is found.

A difficult kind of fruit was usually found
rendered in dark monochrome with mold gone wild.
In her anxious world her remnants ache—
bound by jagged tales that are snagged in the margins,
frayed by foreign princes who want in.
*I'm weary* she says *of trying to force from my mind my subject-*

*ivity*, yet every time the gnomes convince her not to dismiss the subject
at hand. One day a jester wearing a chandelier adorned with flickering candles was found
galavanting around the royal ravine so she had her gnomes invite him in
and with jizzle & gizzle they both fell wild
into each other's percolating margins
vibrating with that ever-after ache.

But pretty doesn't always do, as pretty should, so ache
turned toothy and moonlit pebbles betrayed this harlequined subject
who struggled to catch his breath at the margins
of what she could wield at any vein she found.
Her signature scheme in the geometry of wild
promised him no way out or in,

even though he tried as many *my-what-big-you-have* refrains as he could fit in
her mouth. *My Saggy Stickman,* she cackled, *My Soggy Ticket to Ride.* The ache
creeped out of control through corridors, wild
like kudzu, and the gnomes tried to appease her distaste for this subject
matter that commingled with snail slime and found
its way to her strongbox margins.

So, she had her sway and banished his liver & lungs from her margins,
and he left in bawdy fashion, corralling all his sprightly sauce within.
At twilight, she strolled through garden gates where erect topiary could be found.
Tomorrow she'll order another minaret to offset this feeble ache
and direct more silkworm thread be harvested for subjects
to weave mulberry sheets that serve her kinky and wild.

Again, she finds herself dipped in resin, rolled in feathers and home in the margins
where into her psychiatrist's ear, wild words let her story sink in—
dismembered ache, sweet rot of self and quest to change the subject.

## Believer's Dividend

*Life on Venus? Astronomers See a Signal in Its Clouds*
(headline from *The New York Times*)

The food truck driver likes our neighborhood
and likewise we adore her sweet or savory crepes—
creamy butternut squash, tangy fruit salsa, all
variations that *ta-da* on our tongues. She goes by
Venus, her mother bewitched by Botticelli, now she's
an early evening star making her way in a country
bound by tarnished myth. Best she could, she has
orbited through layoffs, fragile access to health care,
impotent child support. After work today, I tell her
that a powerful telescope looking for molecules
in cosmic clouds has detected in the alien
biosphere of her namesake, a chemical
that could be produced by microbial organisms,
same phosphine found in the feces of our penguins
and badgers. This planet, the only one named
after a goddess, has long been neglected by
most scientists. Too hellish with its powers
of heat and pressure that disintegrates spacecrafts
aiming to tame it. And the two of us bubble
even more as I relay that the astronomers who
observed and proposed this theory calling for more
research, are women. Of course, Venus says, her eyes
moist with memory, her forearms glistening. She
delivers me my nutella and banana classic, another
small victory for survival, but what sticks to my ribs
is her handoff—*You know, belief has been
my divining rod, too.*

# At the Meeting House

after William Shakespeare's *Sonnet 129* and
after Senate Majority Leader Mitch McConnell
at the start of the Senate Impeachment Trial:
*We have the votes.*

*Th' expense of spirit in a waste of shame*
hard on for power, wrist deep in the savory
gravy of partisan pie. Articles honed & cast
deep into the well. Logic at full blast,
rhetoric pulsating, then truth tarred & feathered
by Statecraft, taxonomy of hostility, the carnal
musk of four more years. When lust is in the
longing *mad in pursuit and in possession so,*
joint sessions sour with cardboard comrades,
brackish claims, pungent solicitude.
How to survive the abstraction of nation born
& bred on cruelty & blood, *none knows well*
*to shun the heaven that leads men to this hell.*
Capitol's flag flapping in the gray light of winter.

## Postcard Theorem

Curbside shrub full of feathered lollipops in calliope song,
warm cobblestones in the sun,
grove of bluebells intoning their bluest hour,
soup of questions bubbling in the mouth of a little neighbor.
What time can mean, even more than what time does,
like friendly laundry waving on the line.
We conjure poetic names for wind—*Papagayo, Suestado, Elephanta,*
selfie ourselves into vistas to ensure their air contains us.
How to be befriended
like the butterfly flirting with Klaus Kinski's brow.
Secrets coil to tunes of untranslatable—
fireflies a fleeting, rhinestone feast.

## Fellini's Clown Car

Notice the tenderness
of pandemic
elbows crooked
smiles slapdashed
the lung of grotesque
fruited with loyalties
of the heart.

News nomads whisk me away,
moth wings large as a circus tent.
On the sidelines I fumble for what
I can find in the purse of the day.
Maurice in my ear, I don't know
how, but it happens.

I'm craving bananas—
at the mega Kroger,
coupon comedians
accordion their surplus
into shopping carts,
bounce down aisles
to Muzak's calliope suite.
Miss Tarzan & Miss Matilde
wrestle for the last
toilet-paper 6-pak on the shelf—
consumption a hollow car
we all pile into.

History is seamed with buffoons
who spindle their way
into our world drunk
on slapstick and spotlight.
Yet notice the tender
fables of pandemic—

pantomime's social distance
at a nursing-home window,
so many aerialists suspended
between earth and sky,
a waif's wide, soulful eyes
measuring persistence
of the tides.

## Quarantine Spring

Coldest nights on record
tucking in the impatiens
with tattered thermal blankets
& days with a bad taste that rattles

like cod loins freezer-burned.
Brylcreemed ideas from a dangerous
podium, viscid shipping & handling
my emotions to the front door

landing me in moods for reduction.
The granular seepage of time,
my mind too near to itself.
I am a tiny balloon chasing

its string, dandelions shake their
heads, toss seeds to the squalls.

## Waiting in the Home Depot Parking Lot

From the capsule of my husband's van,
I peer through a veil of windshield
raindrops muting images of so many
t-shirted men carting the heavy currency
of American hologram.  Some corpulent,
others wiry, some wear flag bandanas
or craggy faces that they've earned.
This tattooed guard takes shelter
around pallets, drag on Camels, laugh
at strangers' kids, startle a fragile parade
of goslings making its way beneath
their rusted pick-up trucks with
mudflap girls.. Biding tides of national
meanness, I project our respective
repositories of judgment, our adverbs
jam-packed with *yes & no.*
Rain gets harder, a day's damp tang,
our lives numbed by soundbites & tweets
and the narrow of what we each believe
from our tiny berths.

## Landmark

The train like a wailing pronoun in the dark breath of night
when quarantine responds to quarantine and I ask myself
how do I get from here to the rest of the world
or scale a kinder incline beyond the noise
above this jittery, jumbled ground
my eyes rheumy with incessant news, my lips dry
from the briny kiss of pundits
words gather to call upon landscape
sleep a foreigner who keeps me up under a swollen moon
and I am weary of suggestions for further study
pregnant glossary of regrets
and I am wedded
to my weary couch denuded in its binocular view
the braying train again in periphery
its skein of myth and fable trailing behind
spectral thresholds masked by the winds
a wolverine in my lap
skulls dangle from trees
this tassled place dead air
of press conference somewhere between scorched earth
and uncharted territory
train cars stuffed with under-songs of tarnished narratives
clouds pinched across the much midnight sky.

# Acknowledgments

Many thanks to the editors of the following publications where the following poems first appeared, some in slightly different versions:

*Adelaide Literary Magazine* "Secret Nights on Loop," "Two Windows"

*Aji* "How to Board a Moving Ship"

*Artemis* "Creekside"

*Burningwood Literary Journal* "Well Shod"

*California Quarterly* "When Matryoshka Dolls Take the Runway"

*Crepe & Penn* "Around Our Corner," "Feathers," "Circus Lullaby," "Redux Suite"

*Flare* "'Spring Fashion Modeled by Rising Young Poets'", "Her Self Portrait at Saks"

*Funicular Magazine* "Ode to Time Travel"

*Gasconade Review* "Faye Takes a Breath"

*Hamilton Stone Review* "Hymn," "Quarantine Spring"

*Heavy Feather Review* "Alteration Love Finds"; "Ouroboros," "Pro Bono Messengers in Baltimore"

*Horn Pond Review* "Lineage"

*Iconoclast* "Clown Suite"

*The Ekphrastic Review* "Double Vanitas"

*The Indianapolis Review* "Much Morning"

*The Klecksograph* "Mermaid's Envy," "Sweatpants Theology," "Ventriloquist's Oath"

*Lily Poetry Review* "His Way Was To"

*little somethings press* "Circus Lullaby"

*Lucky Pierre* "Postcard Theorem"

*The Main Street Rag* "Believer's Dividend"

*Manzano Mountain Review* "Dream Recurring," "Landmark"

*The McNeese Review (Boudin)* "What Fancied Her"

*Miracle Monocle* "Weekend Tectonic"

*Museum of Poetry* "Wrists"

*New Verse News* "Day After"

*One Hand Clapping* "Dear Little Sandwich"

*Opal Literary* "Did Icon"

*Pennsylvania Literary Journal* "Fellini's Clown Car," "Lunatics in Ohio," "*Between the lashes of [their] eyes*," "Calculus of Showman," "P.T. Barnum Drags His Feet"*Perspectives* "Her Cats"

*Plath Poetry Project* "American Shop Windows"

POEM "Miss McGlaughlin and the Road to Marvel"

*Ponder Review* "An Almost Ghazal for My Mother's Hats"

*Poor Yorick* "Ginger Rogers' Feathered Gown"; "Stetson"

*RavensPerch* "Catwalk"; "Surrealistic Pillow"

*Remington Review* "Titling My Husband's New Painting"

*Sangam Literary Magazine* "Once Upon a Sestina"

*Silver Birch Press* "Waiting in the Home Depot Parking Lot"

*Stonecoast Review* "Yellow Dress"

*The Westchester Review* "At the Fashion Museum," "How to be a Maven," "Buttonhole"

*Thimble Literary Magazine* "Titan Moving Out"

*Toho Journal* "Enough"

*The Vitni Review* "Now Half as Much"

*Watershed Review* "Mama Was a Big Band Singer"

*What Rough Beast (Indolent Books)* "Primer for a Press Conference Wardrobe" "At the Meeting House"

*Zingara Poetry Review* "Emily May Be Weary"


*We Are Beat (National Beat Poetry Festival Anthology)* "Secure Your Ingredients"

2020 Margaret Meager Memorial Award; First Place; Pennsylvania Poetry Society "Emily May Be Weary"

Lily Poetry Review anthology: *Voices Amidst the Virus* "Fellini's Clown Car"

2020 Beat Generation Anthology (National Beat Poetry Foundation) "Beyond Sliced Bread, The Greatest Things Since"

*Inverted Syntax* (The Art of the Postcard) "Beyond Sliced Bread, The
    Greatest Things Since"

Sheila-Na-Gig's *Pandemic Evolution* anthology   "Mermaid Envy"
    "Ventriloquist's Oath"

*Birth Lifespan Vol. 1* anthology from Pure Slush   "Much Morning"


A selection of these poems appeared in *Head to Toe of It*, a chapbook
published by Kelsay Books.

I am also grateful to have such giving poets in my life who offered their
guidance in the critiquing of these poems:  Steve Abbott, Sayuri Ayers,
Kathleen Burgess, Sandy Feen, Jennifer Hambrick, Mikelle Hickman,
Linda Fuller-Smith, Louise Robertson, Chuck Salmons, Rose Smith,
Mark Webb, and all my Bistro and Salon colleagues.

Also, thank you to three gifted poets, Ruth Awad, William Evans, and
Marcus Jackson, who so generously provided their thoughtful and artful
words of support via their book blurbs.

Much gratitude to Editor-in-Chief Eileen Cleary and her staff at Lily
Poetry Review Books who believed in this manuscript and then deftly
shepherded it to publication.

And of course, thank you Marc for our lifetime of a loving journey
together.

## About the Author

Rikki Santer has worked as a journalist, a magazine and book editor, co-founder and managing editor of an alternative city newspaper in Cleveland, Ohio, a poet-in-the schools, a high school teacher of English and film studies, a director of a student writing center, and her favorite gig—bagel street vendor. She earned a M.A. degree in journalism from Kent State University and a M.F.A. degree in creative writing from The Ohio State University. Her work has received many honors including five Pushcart and three Ohioana book award nominations as well as individual artist grants from the Greater Columbus Arts Council, and a fellowship from the National Endowment for the Humanities. She lives in Columbus, Ohio and can be contacted through her website: https://rikkisanter.com

CPSIA information can be obtained
at www.ICGtesting.com
Printed in the USA
JSHW050438220222
23195JS00001B/20